Are you terrified of sales? I mean so scared you

cringe when you think about it. So scared that you could

think of nothing worse and anything else to do? But you

keep hearing "you need to do sales", "that's the best

chance to make more money" and they may be right.

Sales give an opportunity unlike a lot of jobs out there. It

usually provides a chance to earn more money and get

rewards and bonuses. It can get you things you only

dream of. But as soon as you stop day dreaming about

what sales can get you reality sets in and you freak out.

The nerves come on and the anxiety within explodes. You

decide it's not worth it. There's no way I could do it. How

could I do it? You have to be outgoing, confident and witty to do sales. You need to be able to negotiate and think on the fly, "but I get so nervous I freeze up just thinking about it". Well 'fear no more' because I have the secret for you. The mind-set and tools that you can learn to get over your nerves and anxiety and take the plunge into a career in sales. Not just a career but success! Stick to the plan and you will achieve more than you did in your little day dreams. This pocket book will become your little army. First, it will get you past your nerves and anxiety to find the right sales field for you. Then it will be your little secret weapon that you can keep coming back to through every tough situation you face in sales to

overcome it and win. So... Should we begin?

The first step is to think about what brings your fear

on. Try to get yourself to the point in your mind when

you panic about doing sales then relax, take a breath and

write down your feelings. Find the list of things that scare

you the most. Is it speaking in public or in front of

someone you don't know, or maybe you think you won't

have the answer to a question and will freeze up. In this

process you are going to come up with a number of

things that make you feel uncomfortable about doing

sales and this is normal. There are very few people out there that can naturally jump straight in with no fear, nerves, anxiety and just go for it without a thought of failure. For the rest of us it's different. So find your fears and write them down then you will know what to focus on.

Once you have determined what parts of the perceived sales process scare you we can get to work. If it is speaking in public or in front of people you don't know then there are two things to think about. One, the person doesn't know you so take your self-doubt and feelings of failure out of it. If you get a no who cares, if you freeze up or say something stupid, who cares. The more you do this the easier it will become and the more you will be comfortable with whatever the responses are. Two, practice, practice PRACTICE! This one is key in everything we do but at this early stage in growing as a sales person it is essential. Write a few scripts of mock sales calls and say them over and over again out loud. Read them to yourself in front of a mirror; repeat them out loud in your car or at home by yourself. Then, learn small talk. Learn how to have everyday conversations with as many people that you come across in a day as you can. Start with your family and friends but grow into chatting with people everywhere. Try it when you're

grabbing a coffee, when you're at the mall, when you're

at the gym, try it anywhere and everywhere. This

practice will help you immensely. Then take the same

mindset you used in small talk but plug in your sales

script and try it on a sales call.

Confidence! Now go back to the first part of the

exercise where you thought about your fears in the

moment of sales but now think about what you naturally

like about them. You may not have ever even thought of

this, you may have been so focused on the negative

aspects that you didn't realize you have some natural

sales ability. If you are someone that likes to be social

and chat with friends then lean towards the friendly sales

call and don't go to strong into selling right off the bat.

Maybe don't even talk about what you're selling in the

first meeting at all. Just tell them what you do and have a

friendly chat. The flip side to that is maybe the social part

is what scares you and your strength is getting right

down to numbers. Then you can make a point of being

quick and precise in your first meeting. Prepare the best

most relevant info and data you can and present it in an

efficient manner. Now of course you will eventually need

to blend these two aspects and need to become

proficient in the social aspect and presenting data and information efficiently. But focusing on your strengths to build some confidence in the beginning is a good thing.

Another part of being good at sales has to come down to product knowledge. This is going to vary depending on what type of sales you are in and what you are selling but the one thing that is the same is the need to know as much as you can. Study not just your own products and services, policies etc... but also the trends in the industry and of course your competition. The more you know the better. Every corner and crack in your industry you should study so there is no question or topic you cannot speak on. On that note, study your customers. Research and study in your preparation before every meeting.

The next important side note that can be crucial to success is the type of sales job you have or should be looking for. You may do everything right, you may follow my plan and process precisely but not reach the success you hoped for. This is because of external factors that may throw a wrench in all this. Unfortunately not every sales position provides the support needed to be successful and sometimes the numbers just don't work. If you are in a sales role in an industry that is dying than it is going to be tough to push the envelope to grow in sales. Perseverance is an honorable trait but sometimes knowing when to pull the plug and moving on is the right thing to do and if you can do this before it is too late can save you time and money. Really do your research on the type of sales industry and position you are looking for. If you are currently in a position than audit your own job and industry to see if it has the real potential you need. Find the right balance between support within the company and the right compensation plan to earn what you dream of in an industry that truly has the potential to meet those goals.

Now that you have the right position in the right industry it is time to get to work. Really get to work. You now have practiced your way out of your fears and researched your way to comfort in knowing you can answer any question. But now it is time for the mind-set that will set you apart and allow you to achieve your dreams in sales. In a word it is 'PASSION' but let's get into the details. The first thing that people will pick up about you is your passion. If you are truly passionate about what you do and what you are selling then they will see that. It will make them feel more comfortable and they will have confidence in you and through the extension of that the product or services you are selling. This is not something you can fake. A sleazy sales person will fake it. They will try to give the perception of passion but if the product doesn't follow through or they sway on their morals it will come back to bite them. They may act like they are selling the next best thing but their energy is all built up on the pitch and is not passion. Passion is the key but it is also something that is perceived to be something natural and not learned. This is where I disagree and if you understand this it will help you sell more and feel great about how you're doing it. When someone is naturally passionate what does that mean? Well it means they have an almost uncontrollable feeling for the thing they are passionate for. They feel so strongly about it that they can't help but burst and show enthusiasm.

Passion is contagious and when you encounter someone who has it you can't help but want to feel the same way they do. It makes you feel excited for them and probably gets you a little excited as well. Passionate people are almost undeniable. Imagine yourself as a customer. Now say a sales person comes to you as a customer with the same natural passion but that passion is for the business they work for, the position they have and the product or service they provide. You as a customer are already interested in the product or service because you are talking to them. You, as the customer, accepted the invite to be potentially sold on the product or service or you came to the company asking about the product or service. So as the customer you are already interested in the product or service so the sales person has a basis to go off of. The sales person now explains to you the essentials of the product or service in a way that truly displays that they trust it. They talk about their company in highest regard and may even throw examples in of how great they are and how they treat them and others around them. Then the sales person begins explaining the product or service and can't help but get excited and enthusiastic. Not in a forced way (trust me you'd know) but in such a natural way as if they are trying to contain themselves but just can't help but rave about the product or service and everything and everyone involved. Then they demonstrate their knowledge of all aspects of the industry and can trouble shoot and solve questions or problems the customer has. I am not saying 100% of the customers will buy but if you do this right the reason they don't buy will not be because you were too passionate.

Ok, so how do I become more passionate? Let's go back to the earlier steps. Have you practiced your way out of your fears? Yes, ok so there's nothing holding you back from beginning. Have you researched and found the right fit for a job? Yes, you have the right balance between good products or service and the right support within coupled with an industry that has potential for growth and income. So you have the knowledge to sell, you have the right industry; you picked the right company to work for and have the right position, now you just need the passion. Start with confidence, confidence that you have because you completed the first few steps. You know your stuff and you know your audience. So now start believing in yourself and what you do, make it a part of you. If someone doesn't agree with what you do or like what you are selling don't let it get you down just keep pushing with an attitude that it doesn't matter what they think. It doesn't matter what they think because you believe so strongly in what you are selling that you can't believe they don't feel the same way. You must have the belief that no one else can see what you can in your product or service but you and it is your job to get them to understand it the way you do and see what you see. Wipe all doubt from your mind and don't agree with those who speak against your product but also don't waste your time with them. Believe in what you do till your blue in the face and when a

customer comes along that starts to see what you do in

the product you will be naturally enthusiastic and show

uncontrollable emotion. That's when you have become

passionate about sales.

The passion comes from you and therefore stays

with you. This is a powerful and important statement.

The key point to learn here is that you can take all of the

steps above and transfer them from job to job and

industry to industry. I have worked in many different

industries in sales roles and used the same steps in each.

Now obviously there are going to be huge differences between industries and vast and unique challenges to overcome but you can bring the same passion. I have worked in construction service sales, corporate business to business sales, owned small businesses involved in retail sales online, retail sales and in business financing sales. But in all of these very different industries the one thing I have brought is passion. This has allowed me to be successful at each of them. But you must start the process over again each time. You can't jump from one to the other skipping the knowledge and research steps. But once you have everything in the process in place you can become passionate about your new position,

company and product and service.

Now I am going to briefly speak to a few extra tips

and points in doing sales. This will be useful in

interactions with customers. If you have followed the

process properly you will be accustomed to doing

research and gaining knowledge of your industry, market

and the customers prior to meeting them. But just

because you have all this knowledge does not mean you

should tell it all to the customer. The most important

thing is to listen. Always be listening but especially in the beginning stages with a customer you will find a lot of important things. If you are listening and only interjecting to give relevant information or to ask follow up questions you can very efficiently and effectively learn the concerns your customer has or problems you will need to overcome. If you are constantly talking you will have no idea what their concerns may be. Ultimately, if you don't meet their concerns and solve their issues and problems you will likely not close any sale with them. So don't shoot yourself in the foot and listen to your customer. Listen attentively and take notes in your head as you go.

Be intentional with your time. Everytime I have started sales in a new position for a new company in a new industry one of things I do is get out and network. I try to meet as many people in that industry or related industries as I can. But you have to be intentional or you will waste your time to failure. I have sat through a number of network meetings for business professionals over the years and I have noticed a common theme for those that struggle for profits and sales. They are not quick to the point and they don't respect their own time. If you are familiar with these types of meetings they usually take place in a restaurants conference room or a hotel conference room. There is general time for natural networking and usually a meal but then the formal aspect starts. Each person usually gets a quick elevator speech about their business, what they offer and how others can help. This is supposed to be short, maybe a few minutes, but there is always at least a few time wasters that end up speaking for three to four times the length and don't ever really say anything of value. They speak about themselves and their business as if everyone understands it. Then the formal aspect ends and everyone is free to organically network with each other. This is when the time waster hits the floor. They strike up a conversation with everyone and anyone they can and chat as long as possible before that person absolutely must move on. They linger a little longer to chat with every last person. Then what do they do? Do they dig into research or do sales calls? No, they go find another group to attend and spend their whole day chatting. Sure they have to get some other work done so they spend a bit of time following up or calling new potential customers. But the same theme continues, they chat and socialize. The funny thing about these types of sales people is they go home at night and feel happy and excited. They feel like they have been very successful that day and that they are really making headway. They feel this way because they have spent the whole day talking about their business or socializing with people.

But because they were not intentional with their time they will be the first ones to fail. I have seen it time and time again. It is important to remember that networking can be an integral part of your process towards success but not the only one and should take up an intentional part of your schedule. In fact all aspects of your sales process should be scheduled into an intentional time slot. The successful sales person uses the networking time to connect and learn. Be pleasant and social but don't blab on but leave them all wanting more. Be intentional during your elevator speech and not lengthy. Tell them the snippets so if they want more they can get it from your directly. Then when it's done have a quick chat or two and get out of there. You have things to do,

people to see, markets to research and customers to be

passionate for.

The last point that I want to touch on hopefully

doesn't happen but it usually does. What to do when you

plateau? When you plateau you are faced with a

dilemma. Do you continue on and be satisfied with

where you are at. I think most successful sales people

would answer no. So what do you do? The easy answer is

move on to something else. A new position in a new

industry and that may be the right decision for some in

this scenario. Once you know you are ready to move on you need to act. But before you do make sure you have given everything you can. This is a perfect opportunity to revisit all the steps in this sales process and re-energize all of the reasons you do sales. Stay passionate but get hungry again. Think outside the box and exhaust all corners of your industry to find all hidden pieces of potential you can find. Then once you have done this you will certainly have your answer to the question of moving on or not.

I have enjoyed putting my thoughts and processes for sales down in this short pocket book and I hope you have enjoyed it as well. There are many theories on sales processes but all I can speak to is mine and the experiences that developed them. I hope you use these properly and begin or continue a successful career in sales.

www.ingramcontent.com/pod-product-compliance
Lightning Source LLC
Chambersburg PA
CBHW081318180526
45170CB00007B/2752